Recycled Crafts Box

Recycled Crafts Box

Sock puppets, cardboard castles, bottle bugs & 37 more
earth-friendly projects & activities you can create

Laura C. Martin

Storey Publishing

*The mission of Storey Publishing is to serve our customers by
publishing practical information that encourages
personal independence in harmony with the environment.*

Edited by Cindy A. Littlefield
Art Direction by Wendy Palitz
Designed by Wendy Palitz and Melanie A. Jolicoeur
Cover Photography by Ed Judice
Illustrations by Lisa Adams
Interior Photography by Ed Judice, except for pages x and 52, Richard Harbus/ *The New York Times*;
page 53, Bobby Hansson; page 31, Ela Lamblin; page 69, Anya Liftig; and page 11, Cameron Martin.
Craft Styling by Cindy A. Littlefield
Indexed by Susan Olason, Indexes & Knowledge Maps

Text © 2004 by Laura C. Martin

Printed in China by Regent Publishing Services
10 9 8 7 6 5

Library of Congress Cataloging-in-Publication Data

Martin, Laura C.
  Recycled crafts box / Laura C. Martin
    p. cm.
  Includes index.
  Summary: Discusses recycling and provides information
  and instructions for making art projects from a variety of
  recycled materials.
  ISBN 978-1-58017-522-7 (pbk : alk. paper)
  1. Handicraft—Juvenile literature. 2. Recycling (Waste,
  etc.)—Juvenile literature. [1. Handicraft. 2. Recycling
  (Waste)] I. Title.
TT160 .M2642 2004
363.72'82—dc22
                    2003016703

Dedication

To Jack, king of recycling

Acknowledgments

A special thanks to those people who helped and supported me during the creation of this book: Jack, both for his enthusiasm for recycling and his patience during the writing process; my children for their ideas and support; my parents for their unfailing encouragement for my myriad of books and projects.

In addition, I would like to thank the artists who contributed their wisdom, time and energy in the interviews: Cameron Martin, Ela Lamblin, Anya Liftig and Bobby Hansson. Their words will undoubtedly encourage young artists to use found and recycled materials in their own art. Thanks also to Trevor Williams, Environmental Education Specialist for the City of Roswell, Georgia, for sharing her knowledge of recycling.

Contents

Dear Readers,

On April 22, 1970, a group of college students led an event that would help people all over the world realize how important it is to take care of our planet. They called it Earth Day. Since that time, Earth Day has been celebrated every year. On this day we are reminded that each of us can make a difference.

Although there are many different ways that you can help, one of the most important is by reducing the amount of trash that you and your family produce. That's what *Recycled Crafts Box* is all about. With the information in this book you can start making a difference right now!

It is my hope that as you read this book you will have lots of fun making the different crafts out of recycled materials, and, more importantly, that you will begin to think creatively about all the ways you can reduce the number of things you throw away.

If you really care about the environment, use this book as a first step for making a difference — in your home, in your school and community, and on the earth. Make every day an Earth Day.

Laura Martin

Trash? Or Treasure?

To many people, garbage cans and recycling bins are full of useless things, but for those who can learn to look at trash in a new and inventive way, they are brimming with potential treasures. That's what this book is all about: recycling the items we throw away into all kinds of new and wonderful creations and getting into the habit of creating less trash in the first place.

Using recyclables as art materials is a win-win situation. Since they are free, you don't have to worry about making a mistake. If you goof something up, you can just put it right back into the recycling bin. More often than not, you'll find that the treasures you create from trash will be fun, funny, exciting, and even beautiful! So have fun; and know that while you are, you're also helping to save the earth.

A Cover Up

Trash has been a part of human life ever since ancient times, but back then there wasn't nearly as much of it as there is now. Archaeologists (scientists who study the past by digging up ancient objects buried in the ground) have found caves and houses that contained layers and layers of trash. They think that when homes became strewn with litter, the people who lived there may have simply brought in a fresh load of soil and spread it over everything to create a clean floor!

Thousands of years later, in colonial America, the early settlers used to bury some of their trash as well. Mostly, it was just broken glass and ceramic dishes, animal bones, and pieces of wood. There was no plastic, because it had not been invented yet, and no throw-away paper packaging. Foods, such as loaves of bread that were bought at a market or bakery, were wrapped in cloth or some other reusable material. Food scraps were either fed to the dogs or pigs or used as compost on the garden.

TRASH
start here →
TIMELINE

TIN CAN PATENTED IN LONDON BY PETER DURAN

1810

2 BROTHERS MANUFACTURE CELLULOID REPLACES WOOD METAL AND LINEN

1868

GILLETTE INVENTS RAZOR... DISPOSABLE BLADES

1895

PAPER TOWEL INVENT

DISPOSABLE CAMERA Introduced

2002

1980

POLYPROPYLENE introduced for BUTTER TUBS

1977

PET REPLACES GLASS SodA Bottles (POLYETHYLENE TEREPHTHALATE)

1970

FIRST EARTH DAY APRIL 22

1963

ALUMINUM CANS developed FOR BEVERAGES

1960

BREAD

Now WRAPPED IN POLYETHYLENE NO MORE WAX PAPER

1960

BEAD MOLDED POLYSTYRENE CUPS INTRODUCED Good FOR HOT DRINKS

1959

The Easy Life

It'd be great if all garbage disintegrated the way compost does, but, unfortunately, it doesn't. By the late 1800s, as many new inventions came on the market, American garbage began to change.

In 1895, for example, a traveling salesman named King C. Gillette invented a razor that used disposable blades. This was a hugely popular item because, before then, a razor blade had to be re-sharpened every time a man shaved. Then, in 1907, the first paper towels were accidentally invented when a factory machine turned out a roll of

PAPER CUP REPLACES TIN CUP ON TRAINS AND IN PUBLIC BUILDINGS

CORN FLAKES

KELLOGG INVENTS WAX PAPER ← FOR

KLEENEX INTRODUCED

1907

1908

1914

1924

ALUMINUM FOIL INVENTED

1929

PLEXIGLASS INVENTED

1935

PAPER-BACK BOOK INTRODUCED

1939

extra-thick toilet paper. They, too, were an instant hit because it was so easy to throw them away once you used them (unlike cloth towels that had to be washed when they got dirty).

Disposable products like these sure made life convenient, but they also tended to create a lot more trash than the items they replaced. Today, we're buying and throwing things away at an amazing rate. The result is mountains of garbage filled with many items that are far from worn out but discarded simply because we want something new.

AEROSOL CAN INVENTED

1957

1945

1943

XEROX 914

1st PHOTOCOPIER

HDPE DEVELOPED FOR MILK CARTON

1st AMERICAN BALLPOINT PENS $12.50 EACH!

ANATOMY OF A LANDFILL

NEW POCKETS OF TRASH

OLD POCKETS OF TRASH

SOIL LAYER

DRAINAGE LAYER

GRAVEL

COMPACTED CLAY

GROUND WATER

LEACHATE (decomposed garbage + water)

COLLECTION PIPE

GEOTEXTILE (NON WOVEN FABRIC) MAT

PLASTIC LINER

ALL THE WAY BACKUP TO LEACHATE POND ON LAND SURFACE

Where does all the garbage go?

So, what happens to all those throw-away items? When we say we are going to throw something away, it's really kind of silly. There is no such thing as away. Everything has to end up someplace, and that place is usually a landfill. A landfill is just a big hole in the ground where trash is dumped and then covered with a layer of soil.

While burying garbage and getting it out of sight may sound like a good idea, it can cause some serious problems. For example, the plastics we throw into landfills sometimes give off toxic (poisonous) substances. Sometimes this is in the form of a gas that pollutes the air. Other times, these toxins mix with rainwater that filters down through the landfill liner and contaminates the water below the surface of the earth. That's our drinking water! Besides, we don't want to fill our earth with trash. We want to leave it as natural and beautiful as possible.

How You Can Make A Difference

➦ **Take care of the things you have**

If you care for your bicycles, toys, books, and other possessions and keep them in good condition, they will last longer and won't end up in the trash so quickly.

➦ **Precycle**

Before purchasing different products, look at the containers they come in to make sure that you won't have a lot of trash leftover. If you need to, look for similar items with less packaging.

➦ **Recycle**

A lot of our trash can be used to make something else. This process is called recycling. Recycle everything you can through a recycling center. Most community governments pick up recyclable items just as they do garbage. If you don't know what you can put into a recycling bin, call your town or city hall to find out.

➦ **Reuse whatever you can**

Write on both sides of the paper you use; reuse plastic containers again and again; buy something new only to replace an item that is completely worn out or no longer works.

➦ **Encourage others to do the same**

Reducing our own trash is a great first step but we all really need to do more, like encouraging other people and businesses to reduce their trash, too. One of the easiest and most effective ways of doing this is to write letters. For example, if you think that there is way too much packaging around a game or toy you buy, find the address of the company (it's usually somewhere on the packaging) and write a short letter that says something like this:

My name is (put your name here) and I am concerned about our environment. Our landfills are overflowing, which is not good for the earth. One way we can all help is to create less trash. Please reduce the amount of paper and plastic that you put around your toys.

Sincerely, (sign your name)

➔ Become a Recycling Artist.

Be inventive! Before you put something into the trash can, ask yourself, "What can I make out of this?" It's amazing how many creative ideas you can come up with. Here are some things to think about when you want to turn trash into treasure:

✳ Does an object's shape remind you of something else? What happens when you turn it upside down? Does it look different?

✳ What if you covered it with paper or cloth? How would it look if you painted it?

✳ Can you put anything in it? On top of it? Under it? Through it?

✳ Can you hang it up? Or hang something from it?

✳ Does it come apart? Can you use the separate parts?

✳ Does it make noise?

Don't worry about what your creation is going to look like in the end. Just let your imagination go wild, and have fun experimenting. On the following pages, you'll find lots of project ideas to help get you thinking like an artist or an inventor by using something old to create something completely new and different.

Happy recycling!

PAPER

Paper is one of the oldest man-made materials. Egyptians first made paper thousands of years ago from papyrus, a plant they found growing along the banks of the Nile River. Making this first kind of paper took a long time. First, the bark was peeled off the stalks and the very inside of the stem (called the pith) was removed and cut into strips. These strips were layered in a criss-cross pattern, then pounded, pressed, and dried. Next, the dry sheet was smoothed out so it could be written on. Finally, individual sheets were often glued together to make long rolls. It's no wonder every scrap of papyrus paper was very valuable.

Piles of Paper

We've come a long way from slicing and pounding on papyrus to make something to write on. Over the years, the materials that have gone into paper making include mulberry bark, hemp, cotton and linen rags, wheat and oat stalks, and, of course, wood pulp, which most paper is made from today. Plus, now there are many, many different kinds of papers, such as glossy gift wrap, tissue, newsprint, cardboard, and waxed paper (including waxed containers like milk and juice cartons and coated paper cups), to name just a few. We sure use plenty of it, too! The average American uses an estimated 750 pounds of paper products every year, most of which end up in landfills.

Paper Routes

Every year, billions of trees are cut to make wood pulp for paper. Because trees can be planted, they are called a renewable resource. In fact, many of the trees used for making paper are grown and harvested on tree farms as a crop, much like corn or potatoes. As soon as these trees are cut down, new seedlings are planted to replace them.

A lot of paper is also made, at least in part, from old paper that people recycle.

Almost all paper can be used again to make a variety of new paper products ranging from cereal boxes to tissues and even paperboard used to stiffen car parts such as sun visors and glove compartments. Recycled newspapers, too, are almost always used to make new newspapers. Unfortunately, in the United States, 9 out of 10 newspapers sold are thrown away instead of recycled!

Why Recycle?

Making new papers out of old ones makes a lot of sense because:

➡️ It reduces the amount of paper piling up in landfills. More than a third of all the garbage in the United States comes from paper and cardboard.

➡️ It reduces the number of trees cut down per year, which, in turn, helps preserve more acres of natural animal and plant habitat.

➡️ It takes a lot less water and fuel to recycle old papers into new ones than it does to make new paper by starting with the raw materials.

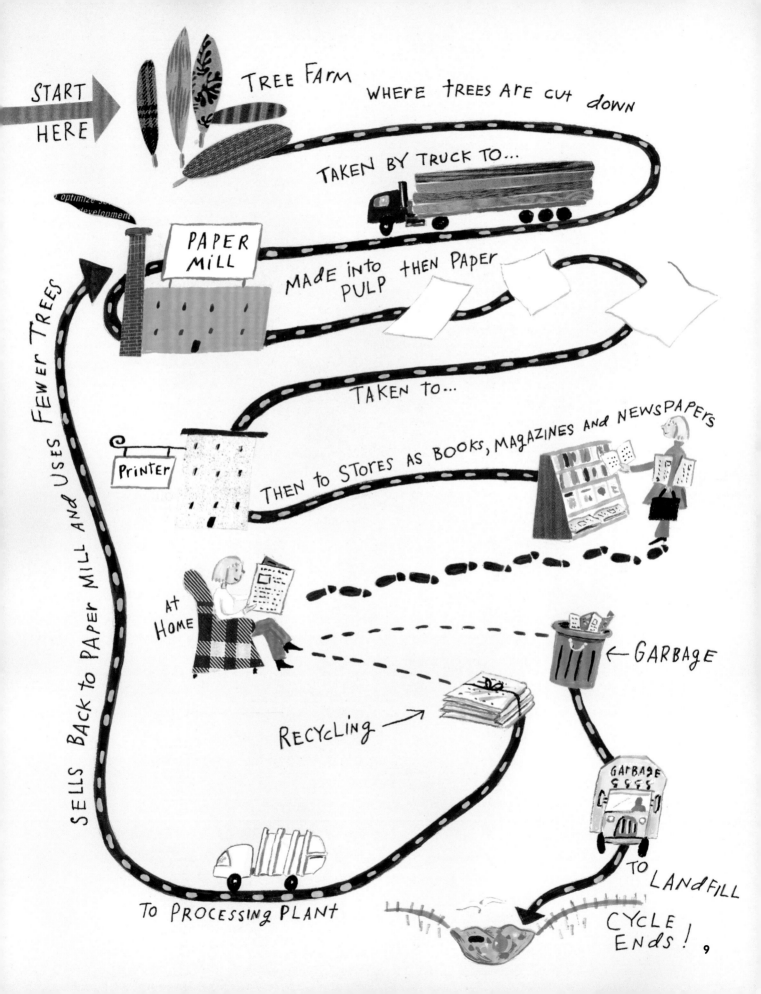

How You Can Make a Difference

➡ **Sort and Recycle Your Junk Mail**

A huge amount of junk mail arrives in mailboxes across the country every day only to be thrown away. Much of it can be recycled as long as you separate it first, since different papers are used to make different things. Here's what to do:

✳ Go through the junk mail with your parents and set aside anything you want to keep.

✳ Sort the rest of the mail into two boxes. Label one of the boxes "White Paper" and fill it with white papers printed with black ink or a little bit of colored ink and

white envelopes without windows or labels (waxed papers and papers with gummed labels or clear windows cannot be recycled).

✳ Be sure to remove all paper clips. Staples, on the other hand, don't need to be removed because they will sink to the bottom of the vat during the recycling process.

✳ Label the second box "Mixed Paper" and fill it with papers that are glossy, colored, or have a lot of colored pictures

➲ Use Less Paper

By limiting the paper you use, even by a piece or a scrap at a time, you'll help save trees, water, fuel, and other resources needed to produce it.

﹡ Avoid buying groceries that are packaged in individual servings. When you do buy paper products, choose ones made from recycled paper.

﹡ Use cloth napkins and dish towels instead of paper ones.

﹡ Use a lunch box instead of a paper bag.

﹡ Bring your juice to school in a reusable container instead of buying juice boxes.

Cameron Martin

For as long as she can remember, Cameron Martin has enjoyed making art. She works primarily with paper to create colorful collages and beautiful paper quilts.

Why do you like working with paper?
Paper is a great medium because you can do so much with it: rip the edges, fold it into interesting shapes, make new paper from old, make sculptures, print on it, just about anything!

What kinds of papers have you used to create art?
I use a lot of old letters, postcards and old photographs to make quilts. I also use photographs from junk mail, magazines, and newspapers. I love using something that other people would just throw away. I hope people will look at my junk mail quilts a hundred years from now and get a feel for what our lives are like today.

FOR RENT
2 Bed Room Cottage

Milk Carton Cottages

The shape of a cardboard milk or juice carton makes it the perfect container to recycle into a toy house. Top it off with a corrugated cardboard or "tin" roof and a cork chimney, and you'll be recycling several kinds of materials at once. The instructions here are for using a half-gallon carton, but you can adjust the measurements to suit any carton you like. In fact, once you get going, you just may want to construct a whole neighborhood or town of different size buildings.

You Will Need:

cardboard milk or juice carton, washed and thoroughly dried

ruler, pencil, and scissors

brown paper bag, gift wrap, or any other paper you'd like to recycle

craft glue and glue stick

adhesive tape

cardboard scraps from empty tissue boxes, old file folders, or corrugated boxes

cork or a rolled-up piece of brown paper for a chimney (optional)

cotton ball or batting for chimney smoke and toothpick (optional)

old magazines for cutting out pictures of windows, doors, and shrubs

How to do it:

1 Cut a piece from the paper bag or gift wrap that is wide enough to wrap all the way around your carton and tall enough to reach the very top. For a typical half-gallon carton a piece 16 inches wide by 9½ inches high should work well.

2 Apply glue to the carton, one "wall" at a time, pressing and smoothing the paper in place as you work your way all the way around. Don't worry about sticking the paper to the carton's sloped roof.

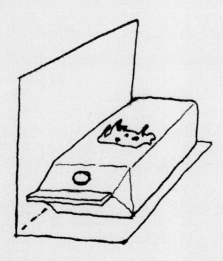

3 Trim the upper edge of the paper around the roof, then glue or tape the two triangular peaks to the carton.

4 From the corrugated cardboard, cut out two matching roof pieces about 4½ inches wide and 3½ inches high. If you want the rippled corrugation to show, peel off the smooth top layer. For a tin roof, wrap each of the pieces in aluminum foil.

5 Place the roof pieces face down and tape the top edges together. Fold the roof to resemble a tent and set it on top of the carton.

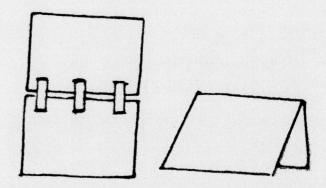

6 If you're using a carton with a plastic pouring spout, ask an adult to help you cut a chimney hole through the roof directly above the spout. Make it just big enough for the cork bottom to fit into. If you cut the hole too big, just wrap aluminum foil or paper around the cork bottom until it fits snugly.

7 For chimney smoke, glue a bit of the cotton ball or batting to the top of a toothpick, then stick the bottom of the toothpick into the cork. Now tape or glue the roof to the carton.

8 To complete your house, cut out magazine pictures of windows and doors that are about the right size for your building and glue them on. You can even add pictures of flowers and bushes around the base of the house.

More Milk Carton Construction Ideas

➲ All Aboard

If you have a toy locomotive, make a train station instead of a house.

➲ Animal Menagerie

Turn different cartons into individual zoo exhibits by gluing on pictures of animals and creating leafy habitats with photos of shrubs and trees.

➲ Interior Decorating

Cut off the top and one side panel of a carton to create a house that opens up. Glue wallpaper and pictures of furniture to the inside walls.

Corrugated Castle

At first glance, a typical cardboard box may not look like much, but unleash your imagination and you can transform any size box into an extraordinary structure, such as a castle fit for a king and queen!

You Will Need:

medium-sized cardboard box

ruler

pencil

scissors

colored marker

4 cardboard paper towel tubes

acrylic paints

damp kitchen sponge cut into small squares

small nail

string or thin cording

How to do it:

1 Cut off the upper flaps of the box, then cut notches in the top of the castle walls. Use the colored marker to draw on windows and a drawbridge door.

2 Ask an adult to help you cut through the cardboard along the sides and top of the drawbridge door, but not the bottom, so that the door opens out.

3 Starting from the bottom of each paper towel tube, cut a slit in the front of the tube that is the same length as the height of your castle wall. Turn the tube a quarter turn and cut a matching slit in the side of the tube.

4 Slide the tube "turrets" down onto the castle corners, as shown, so that the bottoms rest on the floor of the box.

5 Dip the edge of a sponge cube into acrylic paint (use a different one for each color) and use it to stamp castle stones on the walls, under the windows for sills, and around the drawbridge door. You don't have to cover the whole castle; clusters of two or three stones stamped here and there will be enough to create the effect.

6 When the paint is dry, accent the stones by outlining them with the colored marker.

7 Use a small nail to poke two holes through the upper sides of the door and two holes through the castle wall just above and to the sides of the door. Thread one piece of string through the holes on the left and another piece through the holes on the right, as shown, knotting the ends to keep them from pulling back through.

8 For the finishing touch, use a piece of recycled gift wrap or colored paper to line the floor of your castle.

All Boxed In

➲ Create a Desert Diorama

Set a small box on its side and paint the inside walls to resemble a blue sky and sandy ground. From scraps of colored paper, cut out a sun, a cactus, and desert animal shapes. Then use thread and tape to hang your cutouts from the box ceiling.

➲ Build an Indoor Snowman

Spruce up your room for the holiday season by painting the outside walls and bottoms of three different size boxes white. When the paint has dried, stack the boxes. Then use colored markers to draw on a face and buttons, and dress your finished snowman with a scarf and a hat.

➲ Design a Club House

Turn a refrigerator or other appliance box into a clubhouse, puppet theater, or lemonade stand. Cut out a door and window openings. Then decorate by taping up recycled gift wrap curtains.

Shoe Box Treasure Chest

Here's a fun way to put your heart and sole into recycling. Take an empty old shoe box, a few greeting cards, old postcards, or scraps of colored paper, and a handful of trinkets, and you've got the makings for a one-of-a-kind treasure box.

You Will Need:

shoe box or gift box

scissors

used gift wrap, scraps of colored paper, greeting cards or old postcards

small paintbrush

decoupage glue, such as Modge Podge

tacky glue or double-sided foam tape

trinkets, such as tokens, fake jewels, miniature action figures, and plastic bugs

How to do it:

1 Cut the gift wrap, paper scraps, greeting cards, or old postcards into interesting shapes. Using the small paintbrush, coat the underside of each cutout with decoupage glue and stick it to the box or lid.

2 Once all of the cutouts are in place, paint over the entire box with decoupage glue to keep everything stuck down and to give a nice shiny finish to your treasure box.

3 Let the glue dry thoroughly. Then use tacky glue or small pieces of double-sided foam tape to attach your decorative trinkets.

← Shoe Box Treasure Chest

↓ Encore Envelopes
(directions on next page)

Encore Envelopes

Even junk mail has some hidden treasures, like a stash of return envelopes ready for you to hand decorate. Just glue on a strip of scrap paper to cover up the return address and use colored markers to add a zany border or other fun design. Or, you can use junk mail envelopes as patterns for making colorful envelopes of your own.

You Will Need:

used envelope

used gift wrap

pencil or pen

scissors

glue stick

stick-on address labels (or scrap paper to cut out labels you can glue on)

How to do it:

1 Turn the envelope into a pattern by carefully pulling apart all of the flaps. Trace around the pattern onto the gift wrap, then cut out the tracing.

2 Using the pattern as a guide, fold the flaps of the cutout, starting with the sides, then the bottom. Glue the overlapping edge of the bottom flap to the side flaps. Once you've inserted a letter, glue the top flap in place to seal your envelope, and add an address label, if needed.

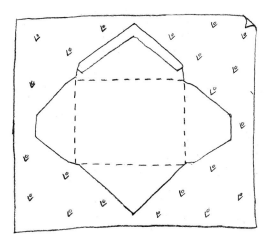

MORE IDEAS FOR RECYCLING GIFT WRAP!

⮌ Cards

Design your own greeting cards. Cut out interesting shapes and glue them to a folded piece of stationary.

⮌ Snowflakes

Decorate a window with a flurry of colorful paper snowflakes. Cut out patterns to let the light through.

⮌ Zany Hat

Mold a few large, layered sheets around your head, and apply a colored duct tape brow band to hold the hat's shape. Then, trim the paper extending beyond the band to create a floppy brim.

Paper Bead Bracelets

Beads for a backpack

Paper Bead Jewelry

Paper Bead Bangles

Here's a quick-and-easy way to recycle colorful gift wrap or glossy magazine pictures into beautiful handmade bead necklaces and bracelets to wear yourself and give as gifts. Or, you can tie strings of beads to your key chain or backpack zipper.

You Will Need:

used gift wrap

scissors

ruler

plastic drinking straws

waxed paper

water color brush

white glue

string or elastic thread

How to do it:

1 Cut a strip from the gift wrap that measures 1½ inches wide and as long as a straw. Working on top of waxed paper, place the strip printed side down and use the watercolor brush to spread glue over the entire paper, right to the edges. Center the straw on the glued surface.

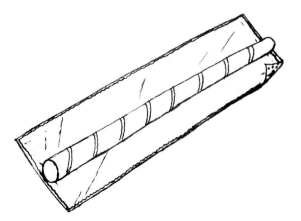

2 Tightly wrap the straw by first folding one side of the paper over it, as show, and using your fingertips to firmly press the paper against the straw and down onto the glued surface.

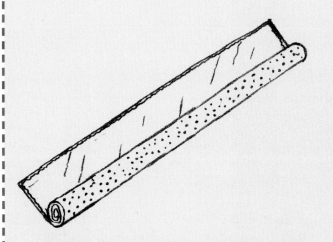

3 Then, roll the straw all the way to the opposite edge of the paper. Smooth the overlapped edge to make sure it sticks well. Cover as many more straws as you like in this way (each straw should make 10 to 12 beads).

4 Once the glue is thoroughly dry, use scissors to snip each straw into beads. Thread the beads onto string or elastic thread and tie the ends together to create a necklace or a bracelet.

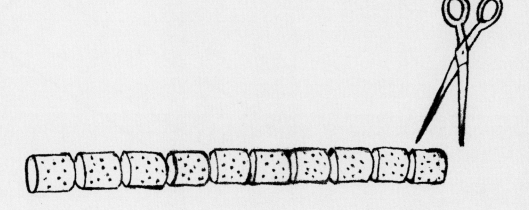

PLASTIC

Imagine for a minute that it's a century ago. There is no TV, there are no computers, and most people have to go to the closest town just to use a telephone. No one has ever even heard of plastic. Then, in the early 1900s, Leo Baekeland, a Belgian scientist living in the state of New York, goes to work in a barn that he's converted into a laboratory. He wants to create a substitute for shellac, a coating that protects wood products and insulates wires. Instead, he invents a substance he calls "Bakelite" that can be poured into molds and, when cooled, keeps its shape. It's plastic!

Here Today, Here Tomorrow

The invention of plastic caused a lot of excitement. Not only did it turn out to be a clean, inexpensive, and strong material, but it also proved to be long lasting — so long lasting, in fact, that it may never go away. We don't really know how long plastic will last. At the time, people probably never realized that so many products would be made out of plastic, and that getting rid of the waste would turn into a problem.

Meet Pete

Today, there are many different kinds of plastics. Most of them are known by their initials because their real names are so long! For example, soda or water bottles are usually made out of a plastic called PET or PETE, which stands for polyethylene terephthalate, or HDPE, high density polyethylene. Another kind of plastic often used to produce take-out food containers is polystyrene, more commonly known as styrofoam.

Cost Versus Conservation

Plastic is made from oil or gas. The earth only has a limited supply of both these resources. When they run out, we can't get any more. In other words, they are nonrenewable. Still, because plastic products are inexpensive to make, manufacturers keep producing them rather than using more costly materials that may be better for the environment.

The good news is that lots of plastics can be used to make new products. Styrofoam, for instance, can be recycled into construction materials, picture frames, plastic keyboards, and CD holders. Recycled plastic bottles can be used to make winter jackets, athletic shoes, and even automobile parts.

Think About This:

Tons of improperly discarded plastics end up in the ocean, posing health risks to sea animals that become tangled in these items or mistake them for food.

By The Numbers

The recycling industry has come up with a numbering system so that consumers will know how to separate different types of plastics. Stamped into the plastic, usually on the bottom of the container, is the triangular symbol with a number in the middle. The most frequently and easily recycled plastics are PET, marked with a "1" and HDPE, marked with a 2. Some communities recycle products marked with even higher numbers. Here's a chart of some of the different types of plastics and a sampling of products that are made from them.

Codes	Name	Some Products it's used to Make	Some Products it can be Recycled into
1 PET or PETE	Polyethylene Terephthalate	Water Bottles	Fleece Jackets
2 HDPE	High Density Polyethylene	Trash Bags	Dog Houses
3 V	Polyvinyl Chloride (PVC/Vinyl)	Clear food Packaging	Traffic Cones
4 LDPE	Low Density Polyethylene	Squeezable Bottles	Trash Cans
5 PP	Polypropylene	Yogurt Containers	Signal Lights
6 PS	Polystyrene	Cd Cases	Egg Cartons
7 Other	Other Plastics	Citrus Bottles (plastic)	Plastic Lumber

How You Can Make a Difference

➔ **Recycle all the plastic you can.**

By recycling, you'll help the environment by 1) reducing the volume of waste that goes into the landfills and 2) saving energy and money used to make new products from raw materials. Don't forget to remove any bottle caps and rinse out containers first.

Think About This:

Even though we may use a styrofoam box or cup for just a few minutes, it will probably be around for hundreds of years after we throw it in the trash.

➔ **Look for the Recycling Symbol!**

Before you buy a product packaged in plastic, check out the triangle on the bottom. Remember, in many places you can only recycle # 1 and # 2 type plastics. If you have a choice:

* Buy eggs in cardboard containers rather than styrofoam ones.

* Don't buy fruits and vegetables that are over packaged. Oftentimes stores will arrange a few pieces of produce on a Styrofoam tray and then wrap them in plastic. You don't need all this.

* Keep in mind that all glass can be recycled; so it may be a better choice than plastic, particularly nonrecyclable plastic.

⮕ Use less.

✳ Pack foods in reusable containers (yogurt cups are great for snacks!) rather than wrapping them individually in plastic.

✳ When you go shopping, do without a bag if possible. Or bring along a cloth bag from home. You'll be amazed at how many plastic and paper bags you will save over time. The next best solution is to reuse the bags you already have.

✳ Ask your parents to consider buying in large quantities in order to reduce the amount of packaging your family acquires. An extra-large container of laundry soap, for example, produces a lot less trash than several smaller ones.

PLASTIC RECYCLING ARTIST

Ela Lamblin

Performing artist Ela Lamblin invents his own musical instruments out of recycled plastic and performs with them all over the world. Some of the instruments are so large he can climb them — or get in them!

What are some of the recycled plastic pieces you've used?
Using recycled PVC pipe and a film canister, I invented the Loonet, a clarinet-like instrument with a vibrating rubber reed made from a balloon. I've also used juice bottles, yogurt cartons, cans, styrofoam coolers, rubber bands and pens.

How did you become interested in using recycled materials?
I wanted to come up with a series of simple instruments made from common items to teach children to make their own instruments. If a child can invent an instrument out of a plastic bottle, he or she might grow up to be the one who invents a way to turn bottles into a bed, or a home, or a vehicle for transportation.

Picnic Plate Flowers

Unlike real flowers, this colorful bouquet never wilts; and you don't even have to give it any water! Making these flower centerpieces can be a fun activity for a birthday party, sleep over, or scout meeting.

You Will Need:

scissors

small nail

assorted plastic plates and bowls

assorted plastic coffee can lids

plastic straws

craft wire

buttons

beads

wooden kitchen skewers

plastic spoons or forks (optional)

plastic or masking tape

plastic jug, such as the kind laundry
    detergent or fabric softener comes in

ribbon

How to do it:

1 For each flower, create petals by cutting a series of triangular notches around the rim of a plastic plate or bowl.

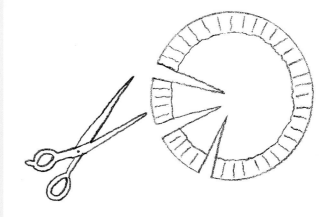

2 Use the nail to poke a pair of holes, spaced about ½ inch apart, in the center of the trimmed plate or bowl.

3 Attach a plastic straw flower stem to the back of the plate by threading a piece of craft wire through the holes, as shown. Then turn the flower so that the front is facing you.

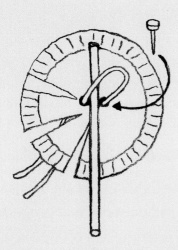

4 Poke two holes in a coffee can lid. Attach the lid to the front of the plate by threading the wire ends through the holes. Next, thread on a button, and tightly twist the wire ends together to hold all the pieces in place.

5 Lengthen the stem, if you like, by pinching the bottom of the straw and inserting it into the top of another straw. To strengthen the stem, insert one or more wooden kitchen skewers into the center.

6 To create flower stamen, thread a plastic bead onto each wire tip and then twist the wire back around itself to hold the bead in place.

7 To make a flower using plastic spoons, tape two spoon handles together, as shown, then make two more pairs just like it. Arrange the spoons in a star pattern and tape them all together.

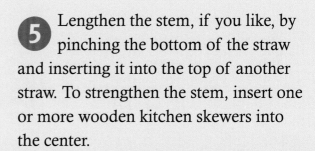

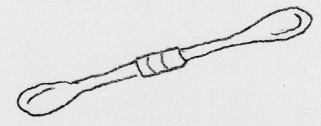

8 Next, poke a pair of holes in the center of a coffee can lid and thread the ends of a piece of craft wire through them from the front side.

9 Set the lid on a tabletop, bottom facing up, and lay a straw stem and the spoons atop it.

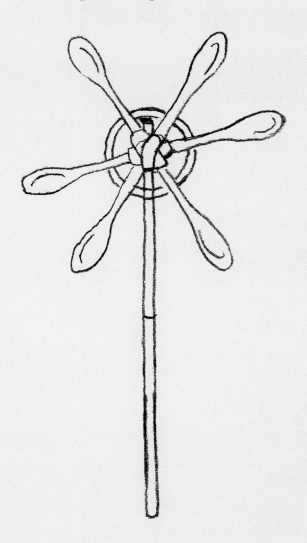

10 Tightly wrap the wire ends around all the pieces to hold them in place. Arrange your finished flowers in a plastic jug and tie on a decorative bow.

Make your own Watermelon Ice Pops!

Empty yogurt cup containers make great molds, and recycled plastic spoons work well as handles. See for yourself by trying out this scrumptious recipe.

1 cup seedless watermelon chunks
1 cup orange juice
1 cup water
blender
3 to 4 clean, empty yogurt cups
clean, recycled aluminum foil
plastic spoons

Blend together the watermelon, orange juice, and water until smooth; then pour the mixture into the yogurt cups.

Cover each cup with a piece of aluminum foil. Then use a butter knife to make a slit in the center of the foil.

Insert the bowl end of a plastic spoon through the slit. The spoon should stand up straight in the cup (if it doesn't, wrapping a strip of foil around the handle just above the slit should help).

Put the cups in the freezer for several hours until frozen. When the ice pops are ready, let them stand at room temperature for a few minutes. They should slip right out of their molds.

Yogurt Cup Girls

Decked out from head to toe in the latest recycled fashions, these little dolls sure look pretty in plastic. Try making one of your very own to dress up your bedroom windowsill or nightstand.

You Will Need:

2 clean plastic yogurt cups

handful of beans or pebbles

plastic tape or masking tape

scissors

double-sided tape

plastic shopping bag, sheet of packing foam, or other recyclable material you'd like to use for the doll's dress

yarn

plastic spoon

permanent colored markers

ribbon

beads and string

plastic bottle cap

How to do it:

1 Fill one of the yogurt cups with an inch or so of beans or pebbles to weigh it down. Turn the second yogurt cup upside down and tape the two cup rims together to create the doll's body.

2 Ask an adult to cut a narrow neck slot in the top cup, as shown (you will insert the plastic spoon handle into it later).

3 Apply strips of double-sided tape around the upper edge of the body. For the doll's dress, cut a piece from the plastic bag or packing foam and wrap it around the body, gathering it at the top as needed and pressing it firmly against the double-sided tape.

4 Make a wig by bunching together short lengths of yarn and tightly tying them together around the center with another piece of yarn.

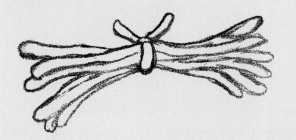

5 Use the markers to draw a face on the bowl of the plastic spoon. Then, apply double-sided tape to the backside of the spoon bowl and attach the wig, pressing it firmly against the tape to stick it in place.

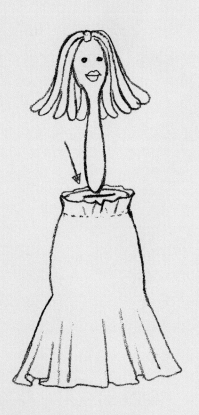

6 Insert the spoon handle into the neck slot.

7 For the finishing touches, dress up your doll by tying on a ribbon sash and a mini bead necklace and then gluing a bottle cap hat atop her head.

Buzz the Bottle Bug

One of the best parts about turning recyclables into crafts is that you can wing it! Just check out this posable plastic critter. Follow the directions below to make one just like it, or adapt them to make another fantastic creature straight from your own imagination.

You Will Need:

scissors

plastic netting from a clementine box or onion bag

pipe cleaners

plastic beverage bottle with a cap

2 craft beads (the holes should be large enough to thread a pipe cleaner through)

googley eyes

How to do it:

1 Cut out a pair of matching wing shapes from the plastic netting.

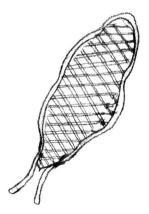

2 Starting at the base of each wing, thread a pipe cleaner in and out of the holes every inch or so along the outer edge of the netting. You will probably have to twist a second pipe cleaner onto the end of the first one to make it all the way around the wing.

3 Twist the pipe cleaner ends together at the wing base. Then, wrap the twisted ends around each other to connect the two wings.

5 Spread the ends of the pipe cleaner to create antennae. Thread a bead onto each and bend the pipe cleaner tip to hold it in place.

4 Set the bottle on its side and attach the wings just behind the cap by wrapping another pipe cleaner around them and the bottle neck, as shown, and tightly twisting the ends together a few times.

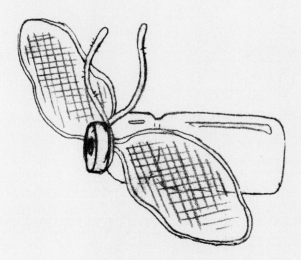

6 For legs, bunch three pipe cleaners together, wrap them around the middle of the bottle, and tightly twist the ends together a few times against the underside of the bug's body. Separate the legs and bend each one twice to form joints. For the finishing touch, glue on googley eyes.

Bottle Cap Shaker and Soap Lid Maracas

It's easy to get into the rhythm of recycling. With a bunch of plastic bottle caps and lids, you can craft a cool collection of musical shakers.

For the Shaker:

small nail

plastic coffee can lid

ruler

cord or thin rope

scissors

hammer

bunch of plastic bottle caps and milk jug caps

craft wire

plastic beads

For the Maracas:

4 liquid laundry detergent bottle caps

rice or dried beans

colored plastic tape

scissors

How to make a Shaker:

1 Use the nail to poke six holes through the plastic coffee can lid, evenly spacing them around the rim, as shown.

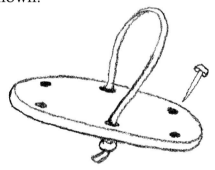

2 Thread the ends of an 8-inch length of cord or thin rope down through two opposite holes in the lid. Knot the ends so they won't pull back through.

3 Working on a hard, flat surface, use the hammer and nail to make a hole in the center of each cap.

4 Cut four lengths of craft wire, about 10 to 12 inches long. Thread the end of each wire through a plastic bead, and then wrap it back around itself. String on more beads and a half dozen or so bottle caps.

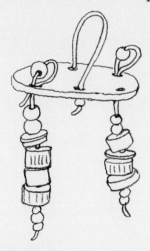

5 Thread the top of the wire up through one of the four remaining holes in the coffee can lid. Slip on another bead. Then thread the wire back down through the same hole in the lid, tightly wrapping it around itself right beneath the lid.

How to make the Maracas:

1 For each shaker, fill one cap a quarter of the way with rice or beans.

2 Set another cap on top of the first one with the rims matched up, and tape them together.

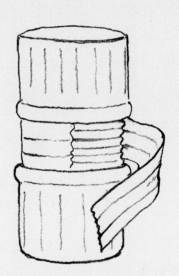

CAP IT OFF!

➔ Paint Pots
Save the screw-on caps from liquid laundry detergent jugs and use them for mixing different hues of acrylic or tempera paints.

➔ Magnetic Locker Lids
Trim a small drawing or photo to fit inside a jar lid and glue it in place. Then glue a magnet to the back of the lid and use it to post notes on your locker or refrigerator door.

➔ Fancy Frame
Spruce up a plain cardboard or wooden picture frame by using tacky glue to attach assorted colorful bottle caps.

Plastic Jar Drums & Laundry Soap Jug Guitar

Made from plastic jars and jugs, these music makers are guaranteed to drum up some enthusiasm about recycling.

For the Drums:

3 medium-sized round balloons

3 plastic jars with the lids removed

long Velcro band (the kind used to bind stalks of broccoli) or an extra-large rubber band

2 unsharpened pencils

2 extra pencil eraser tops

For the Guitar:

plastic laundry detergent jug

scissors or craft knife

6 rubber bands in assorted widths

colored plastic tape

2 plastic utensils

How to make the drums:

1 Cut off the necks of the balloons and stretch one balloon over the mouth of each of the jars.

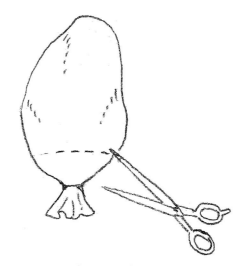

2 Use the Velcro band or rubber band to hold the jars together.

3 For drumsticks, just place the extra pencil erasers on the unsharpened ends of the pencils and tap them against the balloon drum tops.

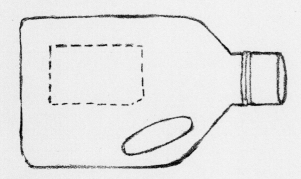

How to make the guitar:

1 Ask an adult to help you cut a rectangular opening in the face of the detergent jug, as shown.

2 Stick plastic tape trim on all of the cut edges. Use more tape to decorate the front of your guitar, if you like.

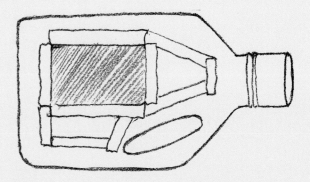

3 Then stretch the rubber bands around the jug and across the opening, starting with the widest band and ending with the narrowest.

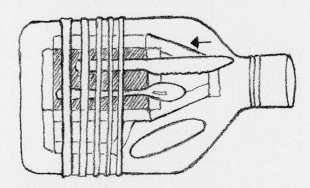

4 Slip one of the plastic utensils under the rubber band strings at the top edge of the opening and the other under the strings at the bottom to serve as bridges. Adjust the rubber bands so that they lie flat without any twists, and your guitar is ready to pluck.

METAL

I f you think metal is a modern material, think again! Thousands of years ago, in Persia, potters used clay that contained a certain substance to make strong pitchers and bowls. That substance was aluminum. The Persians didn't call it aluminum though, for it wasn't until 1808 that a scientist named Sir Humphrey Davy was able to separate aluminum from other substances. Like aluminum, all metals appear naturally on Earth. They're found in ores, a term given to minerals or rocks that contain pure metals. Removing the metals is done through a heating process called smelting. Sometimes these metals are blended to create new substances called alloys.

Here are a few examples of pure metals and alloys (mixtures of metals or metals and nonmetals) and some of the things they are popularly used for.

Pure Metals

Aluminum: This silver-white metal is strong but lightweight, and it doesn't rust. It's used to make utensils, baking pans, storm doors and window frames, rain gutters, airplane parts, and, of course, soda cans.

Copper: Reddish-brown and easily shaped, this metal is often used to make items such as wires, pipes, pots and pans, and some coins.

Tin: This shiny metal is often used as a thin coating (plating) on other metals, such as steel. It's used to make pots and pans, plates, tin boxes, and cans.

Alloys

Brass: This yellowish copper and zinc mixture is often made into lamps, hardware (such as doorknobs and hinges), and musical instruments.

Bronze: Made from copper and tin, this was one of the first alloys used to make tools.

Pewter: Mostly tin with a little bit of lead, copper, and other additives mixed in, pewter has long been a popular material for making plates, mugs, trays, and jewelry.

Steel: This alloy is made from iron plus a small amount of carbon and is a popular material for making lots of metal products, including tools, machinery, automobiles, trains, and ships.

A Can Full of Energy

The most abundant metal on the earth's crust is aluminum, which is found in an ore called bauxite. Aluminum is a great metal to recycle. You can make 20 cans from recycled aluminum using the same amount of energy it takes to produce just 1 can from new aluminum.

Lots of cans are made from tin and steel, too. Americans use 100 million of them every day! Recycling tin and steel saves three-quarters of the energy needed to manufacture cans out of raw materials.

Unmixing Metals

At big recycling centers, cans are mechanically sorted on a magnetic conveyor belt. Strong magnets are used to pick out the tin-coated steel cans; the non-magnetic aluminum cans are left behind. Sometimes, aluminum cans, which are much lighter than other cans, are blown off the conveyor belt to separate them out.

Smaller recycling centers usually don't have automatic sorting machines. Instead, they depend on the pubic to separate out their aluminum cans. This is an important part of the process because companies that buy baled recycled aluminum will reject loads that are contaminated with any other metal; and that means a lot of aluminum may not be recycled.

How You Can Make a Difference

➡ Start a recycling club at school.

Invite your friends to help organize a committee to promote recycling at school. Work with teachers, custodians, and the principal to make sure plenty of collection boxes or barrels for aluminum beverage cans are set up in handy locations. You can even ask the artists in your group to decorate the containers in a way that will make them especially noticeable.

➡ Spread the message about recycling metal

Come up with a catchy slogan that reminds everyone why it is important to recycle, such as: Keep the Cans Out of Trash Cans. Recycling Saves Energy! Use fabric pens to print it on an old T-shirt and wear it often! Or, ask if you can post the message at your community center and other public places that seem appropriate.

➡ **Organize a can collection drive to earn money for a charity.**

Knowing that the reimbursed deposit money for returned cans is going toward a worthwhile cause provides twice the incentive to recycle. To streamline the collection process, see if one or more local businesses will let you list them as a drop-off location; then appoint a pair of volunteers to box or bag the cans collected there.

Think About This:

For every aluminum can you recycle, you save enough energy to keep a 100 watt light bulb burning for hours.

Bobby Hansson

For years, Bobby Hansson has used all kinds of metal recyclables to create unique pieces of artwork and toys.

Why do you like using throw-away objects in your art?
I try to look beyond the obvious use and see if I can discover a new way of using an object to make something fun or beautiful. I think that there are too many disposable things in our world. Plus, we're throwing away things for the wrong reasons: just because we're tired of them or because they're not shiny any more.

What are some things you've created out of recycled metal?
I've made toy trucks out of tin cans, and a lunchbox out of two soup cans and a big olive oil can. I've also made a mandolin-type instrument, which I call a "candolin," out of an industrial-sized chicken liver can. I just use whatever I can find that seems to fit the purpose.

Fancy Foil Fish

Because they are firm enough to hold a shape but soft enough to cut with scissors, aluminum pie pans and take-out containers can make great items for recycling into a shiny mobile of colorful tropical fish, or just about any interesting shapes that strike your fancy.

You Will Need:

coloring book with pictures of fish or scrap paper for drawing fish

pencil

scissors

tape

several clean, used aluminum pie pans or aluminum take-out containers for the fish

small aluminum pie plate for the top of the mobile

permanent colored markers

googley eyes (optional)

white glue (optional)

6 to 8 small binder clips or paper clips

clear fishing line

push pin or tack

How to do it:

1 Cut out several different fish shapes from the coloring book; or draw your own fish on scrap paper and cut them out.

2 Trace around the patterns with a pencil onto the aluminum containers and cut out a bunch of aluminum fish (you'll need at least 8 to 10).

3 Color each fish any way you like with the permanent colored markers. Then, either draw on eyes or glue on googley eyes. Let the glue dry completely.

4 Turn the small aluminum pie plate upside down and attach the binder clips or paper clips evenly spaced around the rim, as shown.

5 For a hanger, thread a piece of string through the upper loops of two opposite clips and knot the ends together. Then hang the pie plate from a hook so it will be easier to attach the fish.

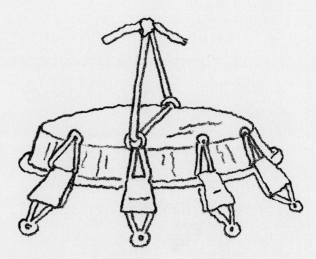

6 Use the pushpin or tack to make a small hole through the top of each fish about halfway between the nose and the tail. Make another hole through the bottom directly below the first hole.

7 Next, tie one end of a piece of fishing line to a small nut or washer (this will help to weigh the string down a bit). String on one or more fish, threading the line first through the bottom hole and then the top hole in each one.

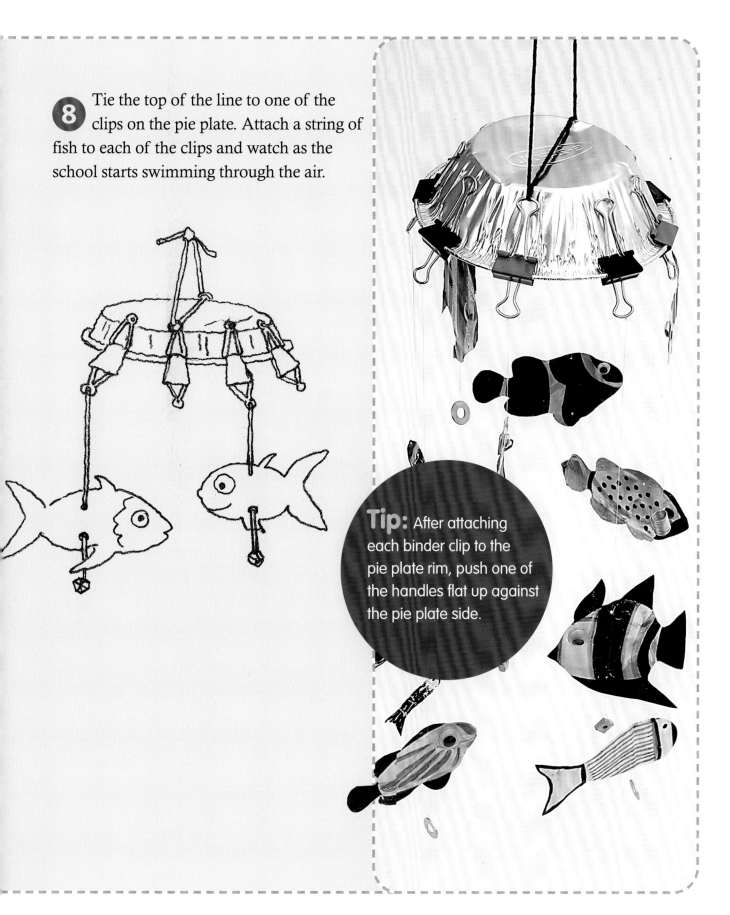

8 Tie the top of the line to one of the clips on the pie plate. Attach a string of fish to each of the clips and watch as the school starts swimming through the air.

Tip: After attaching each binder clip to the pie plate rim, push one of the handles flat up against the pie plate side.

Dancing Tin Can Man

One way to make your neighbors and friends mindful about recycling is to make noise about it! By recycling a bunch of cans into a dangling tin man, you can do just that. Hang him up near your front door and he'll clang a greeting to your visitors, or station him in the garden so he can scare away hungry crows.

You Will Need:

large empty can for the body

assorted smaller cans for the head, arms, and legs

aluminum pie pan

hammer

small nail

big nail

old shoelaces (the longer the better) or thin cord

permanent colored markers

pair of googley eyes and double-sided foam tape (optional)

How to do it:

1 Working on a hard, flat surface, use the hammer and the small nail to make a starter hole through the bottom of each can. Make two holes in the sides of the large can where the arms will attach, as well. Then use the larger nail to enlarge all the holes.

2 For each arm, tie a knot in one end of a shoelace, then use the lace to string together the appropriate cans starting at the hand end. Thread the lace into the open end of each can and out through the nail hole, being careful not to touch the metal edges around the rims or holes.

4 Use a third shoelace to attach the head can and the pie pan (for a hat), this time starting from inside the body can. Tie a loop in the free end of the lace above the hat.

3 Thread the free ends of the arm laces through the armholes in the body can and tightly tie them together inside the body can. Let the ends of the laces hang freely for now.

5 String together the leg cans as you did the arms, and then tie the lace ends to the hanging arm laces inside the body can.

6 With the colored markers, draw on eyes and a mouth. Or, if you prefer, use double-sided foam tape to attach googley eyes.

Can It! More Creative Recycling Ideas

➲ Practice pitching. Set up a bunch of empty tin cans on fence rails or posts and see how many you can knock over with a small rubber ball.

➲ Decorate an empty coffee can with plastic tape or glued-on magazine cutouts for a colorful pencil pot.

➲ Use the open end of a small can for a cookie or biscuit cutter. Just dip the can rim in flour first to keep the dough from sticking.

➲ Glue a gift wrap covering around the outside of a clean can. Then fill the can with candy or fresh-baked goodies to give as a home-made gift.

Scenic Stilts

Here's a fun project that offers a new view on recycling: turning empty paint cans into a pair of easy-to-make stilts for taking a sightseeing walk around your yard or neighborhood.

You Will Need:

2 empty 1-gallon paint cans with the lids on

acrylic paints and paintbrushes

acrylic sealer, such as Modge Podge

small rubber bugs, frogs, or snakes (optional)

small magnets or magnetic tape (optional)

tacky glue (optional)

measuring tape or yardstick

soft nylon rope

How to do it:

1 Paint grass, or any other design you like, on the cans. When the paint is thoroughly dry, brush a coat of sealer over the entire design to help keep it from chipping or scratching off.

2 While the sealer dries, glue the rubber creatures (if you're using them) to the magnets. Once the glue is dry, you can stick them on the can.

3 Now make rope handles for your stilts. Stand up straight with your arms down by your sides and have someone measure the distance from your wrist to the floor. Double the measurement and cut two pieces of rope that length.

Way To Go, Joe!

When Joe Bowen was a kid, he made great strides in recycling by turning a couple of tin cans into a pair of stilts. Then, in 1980, as an adult, he used his childhood talent to raise $100,000 for the Muscular Dystrophy Association by stilt-walking 3,008 miles from Los Angeles, California all the way home to Bowen, Kentucky!

4 Fold each rope in half, loop the folded portion around one of the metal can handles and thread the ends through the loop, as shown. Then tie the loose ends together with an overhand knot.

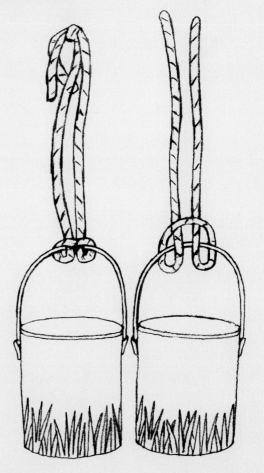

5 When you're ready to try out your stilts, wear rubber-soled shoes for good grip. Carefully step up onto the cans, grasp the ropes and straighten your legs (the rope handles should be taut; if not, shorten them), and begin walking.

FABRIC

People first made clothing out of materials such as animal hides and thick, large leaves. In time, they learned to spin long threads from sheep wool and plants, such as flax or cotton, and then weave the threads into cloth. Because cloth was very valuable, people just didn't have as many clothes as they do today. For example, during pioneer times in America, boys generally had one good pair of overalls for school and church and an older pair for chores. Girls usually only received a new dress for a special holiday or their birthday. Even when clothing was outgrown or worn out, the scraps were used to make other clothes or quilts.

"I NEED A NEW HIDE TO WEAR"

"THIS HAND-stitching ON MY COTTON dRESS WILL TAKE DAYS!"

Stitches in Time

By the end of the 1700s, people had discovered how to weave cloth very quickly with looms that were powered first by water wheels and then by steam. Not long after this, machines known as roller printers were used to stamp the cloth with bright colors and beautiful

"HURRY SILKWORM... I NEED to FINISH tHis WEAVE"

patterns. These inventions made cloth much more affordable. Then, in 1851, an inventor named Iasaac Singer developed the first practical sewing machine. After this, people were able to make or purchase more and more clothes.

In 1910, the clothing industry underwent other important changes that led to clothing that was even less expensive. Scientists discovered how to make cloth from chemicals. Rayon was the first man-made fiber and after that came textiles such as nylon, polyester,

LOOMS AND SEWING MACHINES SPEED Production UP

spandex, and more recently Gore-Tex and other "wonder fabrics." Today, almost half the clothes worn by Americans are made from such materials.

Because clothes and shoes are more readily available and significantly cheaper than they were in years past, people don't conserve them the way they used to. An estimated 700,000 tons of textiles end up in landfills every year. You can do your part to save space by making sure your clothes are either passed on to someone else or recycled into something new.

"AND, produced so Quickly"

SYNTHETIC FIBER MILL

How You Can Make a Difference

➲ Give old clothes a new home

If you take care of your clothes, they will last a long time (probably longer than you'll fit into them). The best thing to do with clothes you outgrow is to clean them and pass them on to someone else. If you don't have family or friends that can use your hand-me-downs, then donate them to a charity. Organizations such as the Salvation Army or Goodwill often accept and distribute articles to those in need.

➲ Try a new color

Give an old jersey or sweater new appeal by dying it a brand new hue. This is also a good way to camouflage a stain.

➲ Turn pockets into purses

Cut a pocket off of an old flannel shirt or pair of jeans. Sew on a long ribbon or cord handle, and you've got an instant shoulder bag.

➲ Learn how to quilt

Sewing patches of your favorite worn-out clothes into a pretty spread for your bed is both a fun and practical way to recycle. If you don't already know how to quilt, you can probably take classes at a local fabric or craft store.

➲ **Donate your shoes**

Find out if the sports stores in your area recycle athletic shoes, which can be sliced and ground up to make a new material used to surface playgrounds and basketball courts.

Think About This:

It takes oil to produce synthetic fibers and chemical fertilizers and pesticides to make many natural fibers, including cotton.

FABRIC RECYCLING ARTIST

Anya Liftig

Artist and photography teacher Anya Liftig has a real knack for transforming old fabrics into new fashions.

Why do you like working with old fabrics?
I feel as if I adopt these pieces of clothing and give them a new life in another context. I think it makes people view old junk in a different, maybe beautiful way. Also, recycled material is free or really cheap.

What is your favorite piece of art that you've created using recycled textiles?
It's probably something I am working on now. I am hand stitching infant clothes, such as hats, bibs, and socks, into a big quilt. I 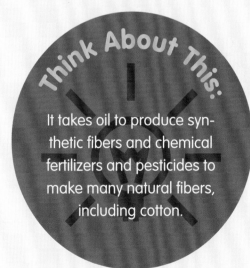 am also dressing up old clothing with beads and other decorative items.

What advice would you give kids who want to create art using recycled materials?
Go for it! You can do anything you want. Just collect a bunch of stuff and put it together. Don't think too much about the final product. The fun part is just making it up as you go along.

Porch Pals

No one says you have to keep a scarecrow in the garden. Dressed in one of your favorite worn-out outfits, a scarecrow can make a charming porch or lawn decoration. Stuff it with grocery bags or bubble wrap, and you'll be recycling lots of plastic, too.

You Will Need:

3 pairs of old skin-toned panty hose

lots of plastic grocery bags and/or bubble wrap

safety pins, or needle and thread

string

scissors

1 pair of black tights

2 pieces of ribbon

long-sleeved turtleneck or shirt with a collar

sweater or sweatshirt

pair of pants

belt or piece of rope

pair of old boots or shoes

baseball cap

old stuffed animal (optional)

How to do it:

1 Stuff two pairs of panty hose with plenty of plastic bags and/or bubble wrap. Safety-pin the waistbands together, as shown, to create the scarecrow's body.

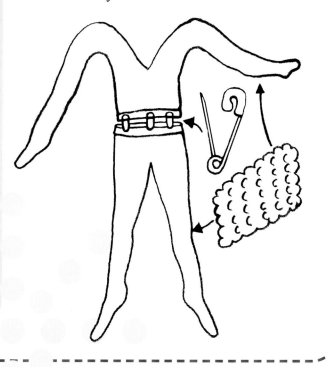

2 For the head, stuff the seat but not the legs of the third pair of panty hose. Then, tie a piece of string around the waist to keep the stuffing from falling out and to create the scarecrow's neck.

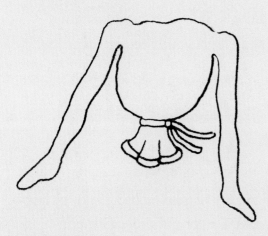

4 Dress the scarecrow in the turtleneck or shirt; then safety-pin or sew the head to the body. Next, pin or stitch the upper edge of the turtleneck to the head, as well (this should make the head less floppy).

3 For a wig, pull the seat of the black tights halfway down onto the scarecrow's head, tucking the unstuffed legs of the panty hose into the legs of the tights. Tie the ribbons around the ends of the black tight "ponytails." If you're making a boy scarecrow, simply cut the legs off of the panty hose and the tights; or you can tuck them inside the baseball cap when you put it on later.

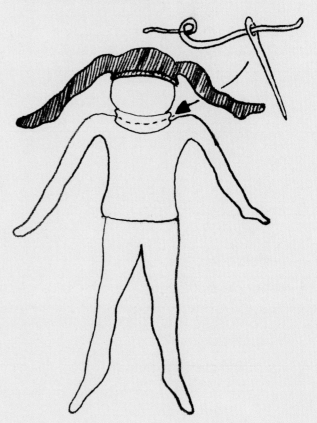

5 Now put on the sweater and pants. Use the belt to cinch the pants to the body. You can also secure the clothes to the body with more safety pins, if needed.

6 Position the scarecrow in a chair on the porch or patio where you plan to display her. Finally, put on her boots and baseball cap, and tuck the stuffed animal in her arms.

Button It Up!

Even when a shirt or sweater is no longer fit to wear, you can still recycle it by cutting it into rags for cleaning or polishing. Don't forget to save the buttons, too! You can use them to do the following:

➜ Replace missing buttons on other pieces of clothing (sometimes it can even be fun to choose a different color and shape for each buttonhole rather than using matching ones)

➜ Stand in for lost checkers or other game board pieces

➜ String onto elastic thread to make a fun hair tie or ankle bracelet

➜ Make a cool lampshade for your room by gluing them on in an interesting pattern

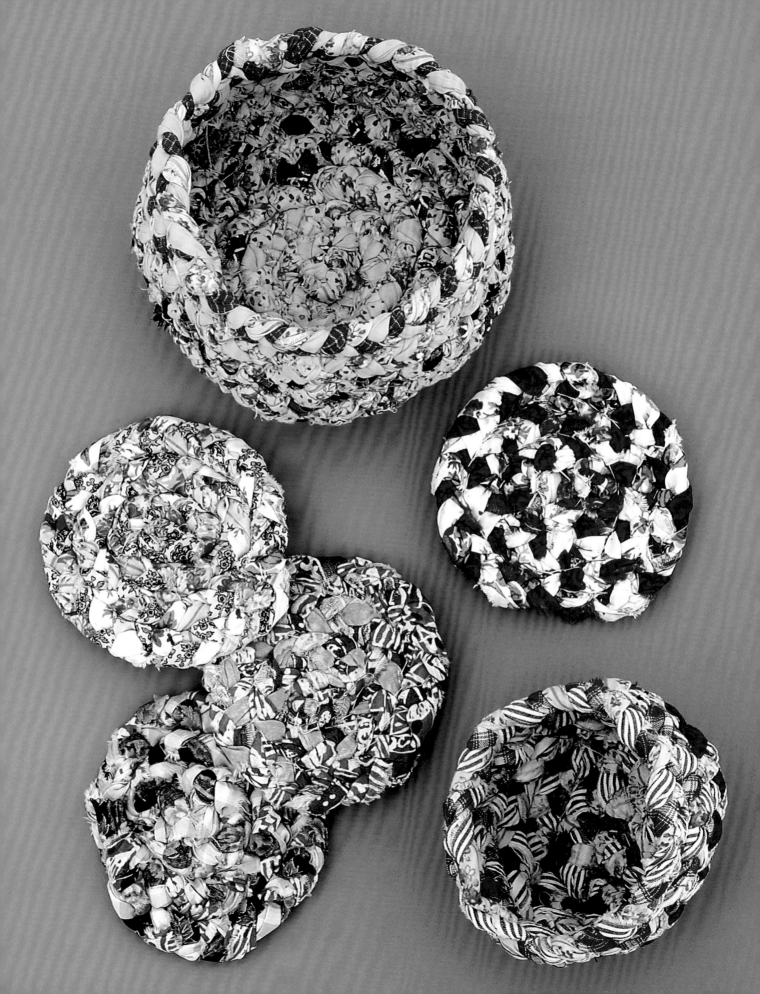

Rag Coasters and Bowls

Making baskets and rugs out of braided rags and strips of cloth is an old American tradition. You can try your hand at this old-fashioned craft using scraps of old clothes, sheets, table clothes, or curtains. Don't be afraid to mix colors. The brighter the better!

You Will Need:

recycled fabric

fabric scissors

ruler or tape measure

needle and thread

a few twist ties

How to do it:

1 Cut the fabric into strips about 3 inches wide and 24 inches long (longer strips will be harder to work with). If your fabric is really stiff, like blue jeans, cut the strips a little thinner.

2 Tightly tie three strips together at one end, leaving a short tail. Braid the strips until you are nearly at the end. Then wrap a twist tie around the bottom of the braid to hold it.

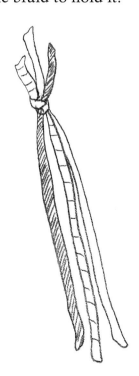

3 Thread the needle so you have a double strand and sew a new strip to each of the old ones with two or three stitches.

4 Keep braiding, removing the twist ties as you go, until you have a long braid. You will need a 25-inch-long braid to make a coaster for a drinking glass or a 75-inch-long braid for a 3-inch-tall by 3-inch-wide basket.

5 Again, wrap a twist tie around the loose end of the braid to hold it.

6 Now trim off the tails above the knotted end and begin to make a coil with the knot in the center. Stitch the rows together as you go by poking the needle up from the bottom through the edge of the inner coil and catching the edge of the next coil.

7 For a coaster, continue coiling and stitching until you reach the twist tie, then go to step 9. For a basket, continue the coil until you have a 3-inch-wide circle, then go to step 8.

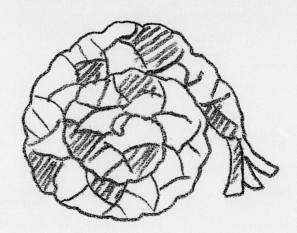

8 Now form the sides of the basket by stacking coils on top of the outer coil of the flat circle, stitching them in place as you go.

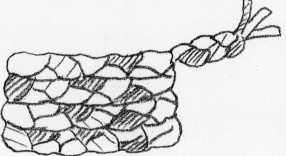

9 When you reach the end of the braid, remove the twist tie and trim the ends of the three strips so that they are different lengths. Continue braiding the strips as far as you can, and then twist the trailing ends so that the coil becomes skinnier and skinnier. Tuck the end between the coils and securely stitch it in place.

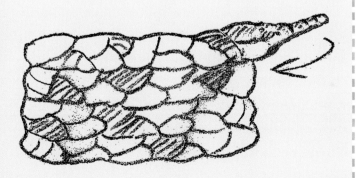

Dress Up a Gift

The next time you're giving a birthday present to a friend or relative, skip the gift wrap. Instead, make a fun gift bag out of a recycled shirt sleeve or pant leg. Just turn the sleeve or leg inside out and use a strip of cloth to tightly tie closed the cut end. Then turn the cloth right side out again. Once you've put the present into the bag, use fabric strips or ribbon to tie a big bow around the top.

A Boot-iful Shoe Garden

Even outgrown sneakers are fit for recycling. Just turn them into a pair of stylish flowerpots. In fact, you can plant a whole garden of old shoes, such as Dad's worn-out boots or Mom's old dress shoes. Be sure to ask if you can have the shoes before you fill them with dirt, though!

You Will Need:

old sneaker or other shoe

handful of pebbles or gravel

old sock (optional)

potting soil

flowering potted plant

How to do it:

1 Loosen the laces of the sneaker and fill the bottom with the pebbles or gravel (this will help the soil drain better).

2 Loosely pack potting soil directly into the shoe (or, for an extra decorative touch, pack it into an old sock that fits into the shoe), filling it to within a few inches of the top.

3 Remove the flowering plant from its pot and plant it in the top of the shoe (or sock). Moisten the soil with a gentle stream of water. Then, set your planter in a sunny spot and remember to water it regularly.

Socks the Puppy Dog Puppet

Made from a recycled sock, this floppy-eared hound dog makes a great character for putting on a rainy-day play. You might even want to invite a few friends over and round up an entire cast of puppets out of different sizes and styles of socks.

You Will Need:

bubble wrap (or other packing material)

sock

felt or flannel scraps

fabric scissors

needle and thread

fabric glue

buttons

How to do it:

1 Loosely roll up a piece of the bubble wrap and use it to stuff the foot of the sock from the toe to the heel. Note: if the sock you're using has a terry-cloth finish inside (lots of small looped threads like a towel), you may want to turn it inside out.

2 Cut out a pair of floppy dog ears, a nose, and a tongue from the felt.

3 Holding the sock so that the heel is the top of the head, sew the tops of the ears to the sock, as shown (when the ears flop down they will hide the stitched portion). Use the same method to sew on the tongue. Then, glue on the nose.

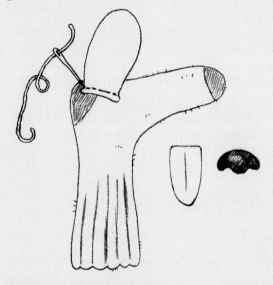

4 Sew on button eyes - it can be fun to stack two or three buttons for each eye.

What Else Can You Do With Old Socks?

➲ Turn them into mitts for washing your bike.

➲ Stretch them onto tin cans to create a colorful collection of handy desktop containers.

➲ Make fragrant sachets by packing them with potpourri.

➲ Fill them with sand, beans, or rice and tightly tie the tops closed with string, then use them for playing bean-bag games or yard "darts."

➲ Use them as mini stuff bags when you go camping or hiking.

Recycling Resources

Suggested Reading

Gibbons, Gail. *Recycle!: A Handbook for Kids.* New York: Little Brown & Company, Reprint Edition 1996.

Schwartz, Linda. *Earth Book for Kids: Activities to Help Heal the Environment.* Huntington Beach, CA: Learning Works, 1990.

Montez, Michele. *Fifty Simple Things Kids Can Do to Save the Earth.* Kansas City, MO: Andrews McMeel Publishing, 1990.

Hansson, Bobby. *The Fine Art of the Tin Can: Techniques and Inspirations.* New York: Sterling Publishing, 2005.

Carlson, Laurie. *Ecoart!* Charlotte, VT: Williamson Publishing, 1992.

Websites

American Chemistry Council — Plastics Division • *www.americanchemistry.com/plastics*
Read up on current developments in the plastic industry and ways to recycle plastics

American Forest & Paper Association • *www.afandpa.org*
Tips on ways to conserve and recycle paper

Can Manufacturers Institute • *www.cancentral.com*
Learn all about how cans are made and how you can join in the can recycling effort

Earth911 • *http://earth911.com*
Search through a list of recycling and environmental events, programs, and organizations to find out what's happening in your home state or town

Students for the Environment (Environmental Protection Agency) • *www.epa.gov/kids*
Interactive games, puzzles, and stories to learn more about reducing and recycling trash

ReUse-A-Shoe (NIKE, Inc.) • *www.nikereuseashoe.com*
Find out how and where you can donate your old athletic shoes (any brand) to the Reuse-A-Shoe program

Glossary

Alloy: a material that's made from mixing two or more metals together or from mixing metals with other substances that aren't metals.

Archaeologist: a scientist who learns about people who lived in the past by studying objects and other artifacts buried in the ground.

Cardboard: a thin, stiff board made from paper pulp and often used to make cartons and boxes.

Compost: a mixture of organic garbage (that means it came from either plants or animals). Compost doesn't last long. It decays and, as it does, it puts nutrients into the ground which help new plants grow quicker and bigger.

Corrugated Cardboard: cardboard made from layers of heavy paper with one of the layers being grooved and ridged.

Fiber: a threadlike piece of a material.

Landfill: a site where layers of waste materials are buried in the ground.

Leachate: water that has drained down through the ground and contains dissolved substances found in the soil.

Natural Resource: something that occurs in nature that can be used to provide food, fuel, energy, or another beneficial service.

Nonrenewable Resource: a resource that there is only a limited quantity of on Earth, such as oil or coal. Once it is used up, it is gone for good.

Ore: a natural mineral or a combination of minerals from which metals are removed.

Paperboard: a thick, stiff cardboard made from pasting together sheets of paper or pressing layers of paper pulp. Paperboard is sometimes called pasteboard.

Papyrus: a type of paper made from the soft inner part of the Papyrus plant stem, particularly in ancient Egyptian, Greek, and Roman times.

Recycle: to reuse something that has already served its purpose, often by making it into a brand new item.

Renewable Resource: a resource that can be replenished. Trees, for example, are a renewable resource because new ones can be planted and grown.

Smelt: to remove a metal from an ore through melting.

Spandex: an elastic man-made fiber that can stretch at least 100 percent and snap back to its original size.

Synthetic: something made by a chemical process.

Textile: a natural or man-made material that is woven or capable of being woven.

Wood Pulp: wood that has been ground or treated with a chemical to create a soft, moist mass that is used to make paper.

Index

Page numbers in **bold** indicate a photo.
Page numbers in *italics* indicate an illustration.

Other Storey Titles You Will Enjoy

Nature's Art Box, by Laura C. Martin.
Crafty kids everywhere will love these 65 cool projects
to make everything from sea shell chess to corn husk
Christmas ornaments.
224 pages. Paper. ISBN 978-1-58017-490-9.

The Nature Connection, by Clare Walker Leslie.
This interactive workbook guides kids to observe
and record what they see, hear, smell, and touch outdoors,
no matter where they live.
304 pages. Paper. ISBN 978-1-60342-531-5.

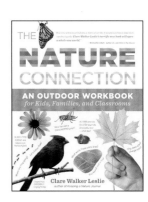

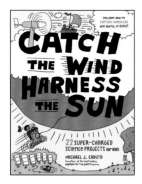

Catch the Wind, Harness the Sun, by Michael J. Caduto.
Introduce kids to renewable energy with these
exciting activities and experiments.
224 pages. Paper. ISBN 978-1-60342-794-4.
Hardcover. 978-7-60342-971-9.

WoodsWalk, by Henry W. Art and Michael W. Robbins.
This lively and fact-filled book will show kids
the wonders of the natural world.
128 pages. Paper. ISBN 978-1-58017-452-7.
Hardcover with jacket. ISBN 978-1-58017-477-0.

These and other books from Storey Publishing are available
wherever quality books are sold or by calling 1-800-441-5700.
Visit us at *www.storey.com*.